Graciliano Martín Fu...

DISCOVERING
GOMERA / HIERRO

EDITORIAL EVEREST, S. A.

MADRID • LEON • BARCELONA • SEVILLA • GRANADA • VALENCIA
ZARAGOZA • LAS PALMAS DE GRAN CANARIA • LA CORUÑA
PALMA DE MALLORCA • ALICANTE – MEXICO • BUENOS AIRES

INTRODUCTION

View of El Teide from Garajonay Park in La Gomera.

A mythical continent, called Atlantis was reported as early as the times of Homer, Hesiod and Plato in Ancient Greece, and was situated in the extreme west of the world as it was then known.

In his book Timaeous, Plato refers to a continent that was submerged as the result of a cataclysim and from which only the highest peaks emerged, the ones that today make up our archipelago. Pliny tells of how the Carthaginians, on their way to explore the African coastline, saw a snow covered peak, supposedly the Teide. Since then our islands have been called Hesperides, Champs Elyes, the Fortune Isles... The archipelago of the Canaries is made up of seven islands, situated in the Atlantic Ocean, to the northwest of Africa, between latitudes 27° 37' and 29° 25 N'. and longitudes 13° 20' and 18° 10' E. of the Greenwich Meridian. The Canary Islands are 1 100 km from the Iberian peninsula. The island closest to the African coast is Fuerteventura, 115 km away; and the one furthest

The sea around La Gomera.

eastern ones, with high peaks, sheer cliffs and many ravines. As they are situated within the subtropical zone, the temperature is stable all year round, thanks to the influence of the Trade Winds. The Canary Islands are said to have the best climate in the world. You can hardly tell the seasons apart and on the coast, the difference between night and day is negligible. Humidity levels go hand in hand with altitude and each island's position, some benefitting more than others. With a surface area of aproximately 7 501 Km^2, the population is of 1 466 391, according to the 1988 Census, a population density higher than that of other Autonomous Communities. The birth rate here is much higher than the death rate, which has given rise to a rapid population growth. Economically speaking the islands can be classified as an agricultural and commercial region, although recently, industry, has made a break through, above all in the sectors of construction and tourism. The air and sea communications both to and from the archipelago as well as between the islands, have enough facilities to ensure a good service. Communications by road are fairly good and suited to the topography of each island.

from Africa is El Hierro, some 565 km away. According to studies carried out on the formation of the archipelago, the Canary Islands originated as a result of intermitent volcanic eruptions that emerged from cracks in the ocean floor. The first eruptions are said to date from the Tertiary Age and the last ones, although by no means the definitive ones, ocurred only a few decades ago in Teneguía, situated in the municipality of Fuencaliente on the island of La Palma.

We should also point out various characteristics, such as the archipelago's topography. The western islands are more rugged than the

On the political side, the Canary Islands have belonged to Spain since the xv century, forming a region that is divided into two provinces: Santa Cruz de Tenerife and Las Palmas. The former consists of Tenerife, La Palma, La

Gomera and El Hierro; and the latter of Gran Canaria, Fuerteventura and Lanzaratote.

If we look back at their history, the Canary Islands were originally divided into Kingdoms or Principalities, in which there was no sole authority for all the islands. Instead, as each one was divided into cantons, they were ruled by different kings, that in Tenerife were known as menceyes and in Gran Canaria guanartemes. Each king had a council, made up of the most outstanding men in the area. Power was inherited and marriage only took place between people of the same caste. Justice was exercised in the name of the prince and trials were held in the

View from the observation point at los Roques. La Gomera.

tagoror. In those times, the islands had different names: Achinech, Tenerife; Benahoare, La Palma; Junonia Menor, La Gomera; Le Hero, El Hierro; Tamarán, Gran Canaria; Erbania, Fuerteventura, and Titeroygatra, Lanzarote.

The conquest of the Canaray Islands commenced in 1402 and ended in 1496. The initial protagonist was the Norman, Jean de Bethencourt, who asked permission from the King of Castile at that time, Henry III, to invade the islands. The conquest started in Fuerteventura and Lanzarote and then failed in Gran Canaria and La Palma, with the inhabitants of El Hierro performing some outstanding deeds. The Crown named Bethencourt Lord of the Canaries. With time, other invasions took place, decimating the

indigenous population. La Gomera offered the least resistance, perhaps due to the increase in colonists, who weakened their fighting spirit. Gran Canaria, Tenerife and La Palma surrendered in the time of the Catholic Kings. The former was occupied by Juan Rejón and the Dean Bermúdez in 1478; the other two by Alonso Fernández de Lugo, the Govenor. After all the islands were subdued, at the end of the XV century, the Canary Islands came to form part of the Crown of Castile.

Roque Agudo. La Gomera.

Chipude. La Gomera.

LA GOMERA

The island of La Gomera has a surface area of 369,74 km². It is situated in the Atlantic Ocean, between latitude 28° 1' and 28° 13' N. and at a longitude of 17° 6' and 17° 21' E., in the western part of the archipelago.
It resembles a circle, and its diameter from west to east is of approximately 25 km, which is the distance between the tip of La Calera, in the extreme west and the tip of San Cristóbal in the east. 22 km separate Los Organos from El Becerro. The highest point of the

Tajaque observation point.
La Gomera.

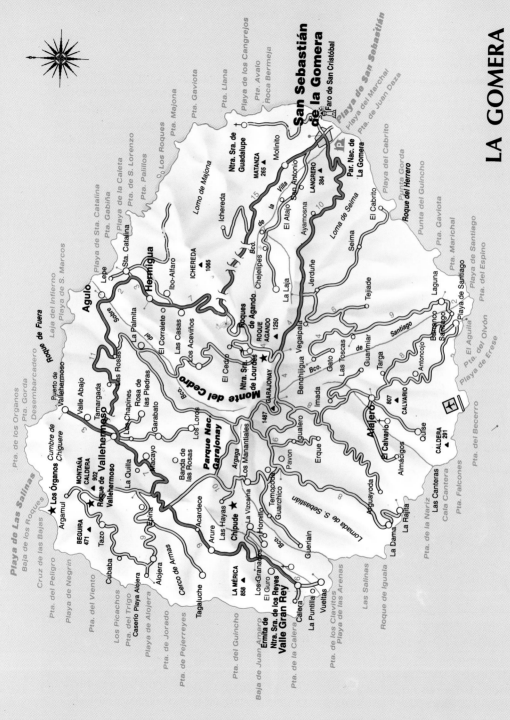

LA GOMERA

ESCALA 1:180.00

OCÉANO ATLÁNTICO

island is the Alto de Garajonay, at 1 487 m, and there is approximately 90 km of coastline. It is the only island of the archipelago which has not suffered any eruptions in modern times, and it therefore contains no volcanic cones or lava flows. Erosion has played an important role here, and its mountain masses and ravines are an integral characteristic of its landscape.

The central area of La Gomera, the plateau, is high and almost flat, and the existing ravines stem from here, with deep, uneven slopes. The landscape is surrounded by important forests: El Cedro and Meriga.

The ravines are very pronounced at their source and taper off softly forming fairly flat hills. In many places they have adopted the shape of a valley and it is here, that the main human activities take place. There are also numerous towers and fortresses, which lend the area an air of beauty and exoticism. As a result of the permanent erosion the coast is steep and sheer, with few beaches. Important examples of geographical accidents are the Fortaleza (Fortress) de Chipude, Agando, El Cano, Jorado, Agulo and de las Rosas ravines, Mérida and Teguergenche cliffs, Organos de Vallehermoso, Santiago beach, etc.

Climate

The climate is very similar to that of the other islands in the western half of the archipelago. Its orography is also worth noting. As it does not have any very high peaks, the effect of the Trade Winds is practically non-existant. It benefits from a mass of clouds which caress the surface, leaving a great deal of moisture with almost no evaporation and confering it the privilage of having the most important forrest and plant life of the archipelago, found in the area of El Cedro.

The vegetation has adapted with precision to the island's climate.

Hydrology

La Gomera has not been lavished with water galleries, but it does contain many springs. The existence of aquifers is a result of the vertical erosion of the ravines. Some areas harbour streams that have still not been channeled, and the building of wells and dams is common practice here. The dams in existence are the most important ones of the archipelago. However, the drought here is also beginning to be felt, in spite of possessing a considerable flow of water, placing it in fourth position after Tenerife, Gran Canaria and La Palma, receiving about 15 hm^3 of rainfall.

Vegetation

The vegetation is diverse at each of the levels that make up the island. It has the greatest variety of laurisilva (wet forrest, predominant in the Mediteranean area during the Terciary Age) in the Canary Islands, with some eighteen different species, and is also home to numerous palm trees.

Working your way up from the coast to the summit, you will see that the

*La Guancha
ravine.*

Malfurada.

Owl.

Cardón.

former has many thistles and tabaibales (a typical Gomeran plant). In the areas suitable for agriculture and cattle raising, there has been a decrease in these activities. Various species have started to grow, with the balo and sweet tabaiba predominating. In between the coast and the forrest, palm trees thrive, in particular the Canary palm; there are also sabinares, jarales (typical trees from this area), and some dragon trees. The forrest is made up of laurisilva and fayal-brezal

Banana plantations in Hermigua.

(similar to heather). Monteverde is both a typical and diverse plant, found mainly around El Cedro basin, home to the best specimens in the whole of the Canary Islands. Because of this it has been granted the priviledge of being declared a National Park. The existing pine forrests are the fruit of succesive reaforrestation, for it is thought that originally there were no areas of pine trees growing on the island, due perhaps to the absence of lava flows. Examples: barrullo, white sage, everlasting flowers, balsam, the holy tree of "Epina", Magaña dragon tree, etc.

Fauna

The island is home to a great variety of creatures, with many different species of insects (Coleopterons) and various lizards, such as the tizón. Regarding birds, there is the rabiche dove, guirres, aguilillas (a type of small eagle) guinchos, and sparrow hawks, to name but a few. There are also many canaries, pintos, corujas, frailescos (typical birds from the area), blackbirds, kestrels, etc.

Economy

The economy in Gomera has been based on agriculture and cattle raising, with an increase in fishing. As a result of the springs, irrigation farming is the most common method of cultivation, in spite of the fact that there are no large areas of agricultural land. Instead, the spaces created by terracing, a method which is necessary due to the unevenness of the orography, are used to the full. Important products are bananas and in second place,

Vallehermoso beach. La Gomera.

tomatoes. The potato is very important as a subsistence crop.

The island has an abundance of palm trees, and from their sap, known as "guarapo" (sugar cane), palm tree honey is made. Date palms are also important.

The most common practice in agriculture, is to own very small farms, plots of land or to share-crop.

Nowadays, cattle raising barely affects the island's economy at all, and is mainly geared towards consumption within the island. Due to the protection given to the mountains, cattle raising has decreased.

Fishing is quite important, but the fleet

Santiago beach.

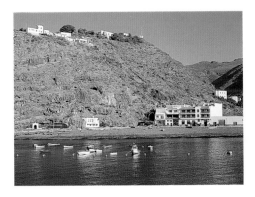

15

and implements are old fashioned. Due to the perilous interior road network, until just over five years ago, in the past many places were connected by sea, through the use of launches. Now maritime communications are excellent, with both a ferry service and jet foil. An airport has being planned, but this will be very difficult to carry through because of the island's orography.

Tourism

Tourism in La Gomera has been practically non-existant. It has increased lately, as a result of   - improvements in the connections by sea, but not to the extent that it deserves. Tourists who come to Colombina Island, do so mainly because of the beauty of the landscape, rather than for any other activity that is characteristic of tourist areas. Some outstanding places are: la Villa, Santiago beach, Valle Gran Rey, etc.

Population

One of the predominant characteristics of the population is that it is very dispersed. La Gomera is the island with the greatest number of settlements in relation to the number of inhabitants of the archipelago. These settlements are concentrated in four large ravines or valleys, Hermigua, la Villa, Vallehermosa and Valle Gran Rey, mainly because of the availability of water and the fact that they are favourable areas in which to settle. Before the 1950's, there was a marked increase in the population however, for various reasons, it decreased significantly, with a population in 1981 of 18257, which worked out at 50 inhabitants per square kilometre. Emigration has been the cause of depopulation; emigration due to scarce economic resources, isolation, bad communications and the physical geography of the island. Many places have aged, as the young people have left in search of a brighter future. Tenerife has been the spot favoured by the people of Gomera, because of the expansion of its metropolitan areas and agricultural regions. Places such as Taco, in the municipality of San Cristóbal de La Laguna; or El Fraile, Guaza, Fañabé, La Camella, Chío, Alcalá, San Juan beach in the south of the island, amongst others, have seen the arrival of people from Gomera.

Crafts

In the past, craftsmanship was of well known importance, but nowadays it has tended to disappear. The precarious economy has gone hand in hand with a lack of industry. However, there are still various artists on the island that base their work on the raw materials at hand. From the palm tree, beautiful basketwork is obtained, located at Valle Gran Rey and Vallehermoso, where you can also find matting, brushes, hats, etc. Basketwork made from dark wicker is made in Macayo, Hermigua and Agulo, where trays and small baskets are on display. Hermigua and Agulo are two municipalities with excellent woodwork and leather handicrafts, making miniture farming tools, pottery, leather bags and drums, amongst other things. Many different objects are made in the north of the island and Valle Gran Rey, where the banana trees are used as the raw material. Cloth and pottery, made in the old fashioned style, as it used to be originally, is produced in Alajeró, Vallehermoso and Hermigua and Valle Gran Rey. In the textile mills in Hermigua, you can still see the old machinery used by the women, which has been lovingly preserved. There is a museum in this village in which numerous implements collected by a great man, Virgilio Brito, who loved his land dearly, are on display.

El Cercado, Cipude, Arure..., centres that live and breathe the craftsmanship tradition, which is like the umbilical cord of a centuries old story, sustaining the desire to continue to show the methods and ways of the best craftsmanship.

Folklore

Dancing and singing have always been the way in which the villagers have expressed their feelings. Like all the others, Columbina Island, has enthusiastically preserved the old traditions, in spite of the inluence, in this case negative, of progress. Apart from the isa, folía and malagueña dances, similar to those found on the other islands, it has also kept alive an ancestral song and dance, peculiar to Gomera: the Gomeran tajaraste or

Above: Gomeran whistle. Below: A gomeran with an "astia" or wooden pole.

dance of the drum. It is basically a series of short, rythmical, characteristic steps, danced in time to the beat of drums and chácaras, whilst the choir repeats a verse after each intervention by the soloist. The Gomeran tarjaste can last quite a long time, depending purely on the participants. It is not known how it arrived on the island, but is still alive today, thanks to a distinguished and outstanding folklorist, Lilí Ascanio, who with goodwill, and in spite of the difficulties involved, is director of the "Coros y Danzas" (Choirs and Dances) of Hermigua-Agulo, the greatest exponents of this type of song and dance. Another form of expression which should be mentioned are the Décimas or Puntos Cubanos, accompanied by a lute or guittar, but in which no dancing is involved. Legends, historical or cultural events are narrated in the décimas", and one of their characteristics is that they are improvised.

Art

In this section, which is always important, as it marks the peoples development and evolution, we will start with the pre-history of the former dwellers, where Art existed in accordance with the way of life, for the objects found had a functional rather than artistic use. The sedentary way of life led to the practice of agricultural work, using equipment that was appropriate and limited to the task in hand, as the resources available were very scarce. Transhumance also existed, as pastures were not found all over the island, but were more abundant in areas constantly affected by the Trade Winds. The valleys and ravines might be veritable graveyards of treasures that could enable us to form a clearer picture of the lives of the former dwellers. However, with the harsh and rugged terrain and difficult access to some places, this opinion may not stand. But agriculture and farming were not the only ways in which the islanders earnt their living. Many of them moved temporarily to other areas, in search of other forms of subsistance and ways to make the most of what was available. Regarding primitive dwellings, apart from the use of caves, such as the Conde or Iballa caves, they lived in circular huts. Various places worth mentioning are, Arguamul, Fortaleza de Chipude (Chipude Fortress)...

Pottery, as a means of identity of a people, is almost unknown. Only a few fragments have been found, with no writing comparable to that found on objects discovered in Tenerife. The pots found are similar to wooden ones, with concave bases and curved handles. The discovery to date of cave paintings has been scarce.

Once in the period of conquest and subsequent years, we find many different styles on the island. We will start with Gothic art which was introduced mainly by the Portuguese. They established and interpreted the most important elements of the

*The parish of la Asunción
in San Sebastián de la Gomera.*

manuelino style (an architectural style prevalent in Portugal during the reign of Manuel I): bust moulds, splayed skylights, etc. The most outstanding example of this style is the parish church of Nuestra Señora de la Asunción (Our Lady of the Assumption), situated in the capital of the island, and which belongs to the middle period. Other examples in what is religous architecture are the hermitage of San Sebastián (St. Sebastian), in la Villa, and the church of the ex-convent of San Pedro Mártir (St. Peter the Martyr), in Hermigua. An example of this style in secular architecute is the Torre del Conde

(Count's tower), in San Sebastián de La Gomera.
There are few buildings worth mentioning that date back to the Renaissance period. Two examples are the church of El Salvador (the Saviour) in Alajeró and a pilaster in the church of the Asunción, in la Villa.
Examples of Barroque art can be found in the church of Nuestra Señora de la Asunción.
Paintings and sculptures are of some importance, with pictures, altarpieces, etc., in the chapel of San Sebastián,

church of the Asunción, churches of Santo Domingo de Guzmán and the Encarnación (Incarnation) (Hermigua), parrishes of Chipude and Alajeró...

As occured with the aforementioned periods, the neoclassic and subsequent periods were not introduced to the island in a strong way, but they did have the influence that they deserved. However, on some occasiones you can see a lack of consistancy in the various spheres and specimens of workmanship.

Leaving this type of art to one side, we come to the silbo (whistle), which rather than linguistics as such, is more an important, characteristical and folkloric form of expression.

The silbo is a form of communication that has been preserved since the pre-hispanic period. It can be said that it is almost unique in the world, with the exception of an indian tribe in Mexico. It is a language of articulated whistles, and arose due to the orography of the island and the lack of a good communications network, which was not developed until well into the 20th century. It is said to come from Africa, brought to the island by the immigrants that arrived before the conquest. The silbo, according to Professor Ramón Trujillo, "is simply a mechanism that substitues oral language, such as writing, the Morse Code, etc. Describing it graphically, we can say that it is a type of "immitation" of the common language; and regarding its structure, it is obvious that it does not possess its own particular personality, as it is purely a long-range transmission mechanism of the spoken language. Therefore it is credible that it was used by the pre-hispanic inhabitants of La Gomera to communicate in their language, being adapted to Spanish later on...

History

The origins of the name, La Gomera, have been hotly disputed, although it is believed to be of Berber origin, in particular from Mauritania. However, Antonio de Viana maintained that it may have come from Gomer, grandson of Noah, son of Japheth, a prince and conqueror of this atlantic isle, and who it was named after in honour of his heroic deeds. Others, such as Nebrija, believe that it is derived from the name of the first African settlers, called Gomeros or Gomeritas, inhabitants of the Mauritanian hills. It could also be that the first European discoverers baptised it without consulting the natives. Another theory is that a Conqueror called Gómez, gave it his name. Abréu Galindo attributes it to the Mastic tree, which grows all over the island and is famous for its goma (rubber), after which it was named by the Spaniards from the Old Continent. The naturalist and writer Pliny called it Junonia Menor.

The inhabitants of Colombina Island were dark skinned, of medium height, strong, agile and very brave. They were well suited to gymnastics. They stood out as great warriors, as they were trained for this practically since birth.

As regards their language, although rough, they were clear when they spoke and perhaps the silbo was their best means of oral communication. Their diet was simple. They used grain to make flour, and also made the most of the plants available. Fruit was wild: dates, blackberries, pine cones and palm hearts, etc. They liked raw meat, which was always accompanied with some other food. They were good swimmers, which enabled them to catch fish and shellfish. When they felt like a drink they had guarapo (sugar-cane), made from palm tree sap.

The clothes they wore, were tamarcos, a type of dress coat, that covered them from their neck, to half way down their legs and which they dyed red, purple or blue. They extracted these dyes from the roots of the tajinaste, yerba pastel or other plants. The womens clothes were made from sheepskin; they decorated their heads with headdresses made from the softest fur, which hung down to their shoulders, and used pigskin sandals as shoes. They were troglodytes, for the natural caves were used as homes. They had a fair amount of cattle which grazed on the hills. In the social world, their rules on inheritance are the most interesting. They believed that the male was the depository of the property in marriage and when he died it was his sister and not his children who inherited it. Regarding sovereignty, the island was divided into four sections and each one had a chief. However, it is possible that there was also a fifth chief, who as the wisest one among them, was consulted by all the others. It is said that the great chief of these Gomeran kings was Hupalupa, according to the episode in the Baja del Secreto. The tribal chiefs acquired such status as a result of their heroic deeds in war.

As regards the religous aspect, they believed in a god who they called Orahan, and a devil: Hirguan. Fortune-tellers and wise men were very important among the Gomerans. Worship and sacrifices were practised in the highlands. At death, the Gomerans used the natural caves as tombs and if where death befell them tombs were scarce, they dug open air graves and then covered the body with stone slabs.

At the time of the conquest, Junonia Menor was only a kingdom. the ruler at the time was Prince Amalahuige, who was later to be called Fernando, at the wishes of Fernando Ormel, from Galicia, who with his tactics, obtained a

Torre del Conde (Count's Tower), in San Sebastián de La Gomera.

great deal from the noble Guanche (name given to the people who lived in the Canary Islands, before the XV Century). After the death of King Amalahuige, and as a result of a civil war, the island was divided into four cantons. Fernando Aberbequeye in Mulagua; Fernando Alguabozegue in Agana; Pedro Auhagal in Ipalán and Meteguanchepe in Orone. This division weakened the island and was a good weapon in the hands of the conquerors, who were under the orders of Juan de Bethencourt. He had no problem in subduing the island, for the Spaniards had already invaded by the end of the XIV century, forcing the kings and their vassals to be baptised. As the Gomerans wanted peace, they were well treated, with the exception of the rebels who stalked the hills. The conqueror took property and lands for his soldiers and built a fortress.

With time, the island was passed on to the Count of Niebla; later on, in 1430, Guillén de las Casas ruled in the name of the King of Castile. In 1445, Fernán Peraza the Old, took over, for he was married to Inés de las Casas, and fixed his residence in La Gomera. After his death in Benahoare (La Palma) he was suceeded by Diego de Herrera, who married Mistress Inés. Upon her death, her children became the heirs, and La Gomera went to Fernán Peraza the Younger. Due to the nobles opression of the natives, the latter rebeled against the authorities. They wanted to depend more on the rulers of the peninsular than on the nobles, because of the high taxes imposed opon them by these men. As a result of these revolts hundreds of Gomerans were killed. Fernán Peraza the Younger's bitter nature, aroused the hatred of his subjects. He ordered the murder of Juan Rejón due to old quarrels they had had in the raids during the conquest of Gran Canaria. He was ordered back to the peninsula because of this, but was not found guilty because of strong family influences. Queen Isabella ordered him to marry a maiden from the court, Beatriz de Bobadilla, who was possibly courted by King Ferdinand.

Now, however, it was not only Peraza's attitude that bothered the Gomerans, but Beatriz's too, which was why, in succesive rebellions, they had to take refuge in the tower and ask Pedro de Vera for help. This episode ended with the slavery and death of the Gomeran leaders, but the idea of killing Peraza the Younger never left the natives minds. They conspired against him and asked Hupalupa and Hautacuperche for help. The tragic death of Peraza took place in the canton of Mulagua, in a cave he had gone to, to meet up with the beautiful Iballa. Once they learned of his death, the Gomerans rebelled again against the despotic rule, and Beatriz de Bobadilla had to take refuge in the tower once more. Pedro de Vera, governor of Gran Canaria was asked for help yet again and on hearing of the arrival of reinforcements, the Gomerans took refuge in the hills of Garajonay. The Gomeran nobility betrayed them

and after false promises by the conquerors, were practically wiped out, many of them hung or deported. A cross, known as the Horca (Gallows), situated on the cliff of Hila, in San Sebastián, is a reminder of this horrible episode. Bishop Frías complained to the Catholic Kings about what had occured and Pedro de Vera was summoned to Court. After this occupation, the new settlers that arrived on Colombina Island, forced the Gomerans to live as outcasts, and they were consequently deprived any possibilities of proper education.
At the end of the XV century, La Gomera, as occured to the rest of the islands of the archipelago, was attached to the Crown of Castile.

Gastronomy
La Gomera, like all of the archipelago's islands, has its own culinary delights. The most simple dish is the gofio (toasted, ground maize) which can be complemented with other good food, such as palm tree honey. Another dish is the baifo barrado, pork with stewed potatos or papas arrugadas (boiled potatoes with the skin left on so they wrinkle), . Fish is also eaten with potatos: white, blue, or salted fish... The shellfish eaten is roast or pickled limpet. Meals are usually accompanied with a good mojo (mojo picón is a typical spicy sauce made in the Canary Islands), such as one that is made with coriander or almogrote. You should also try sancocho (stew made of meat, yucca, bannanas and other ingredients) and yam stew, watercress stew, etc. The desserts include curd and fern tarts, roasted milk, macaroons... Drinks worth trying are the gomerón, mojito gomero (contains rum, sugar, lemon and mint), palmardiente and burrito. There are a few white wines and a greater number of red wines.

MUNICIPALITIES

San Sebastián de la Gomera

With a surface area of 113,59 km^2 and a population of 5 586 inhabitants, it is the capital of the island, and the second largest municipality. It changes dramatically depending on where you are. The area of La Dehesa (meadow) de Majona, which was previously an area of pasture land, is currently in a state of abandonment. At the highest point of the ravine of la Villa, there are various hamlets, and the coastal area has been somewhat devloped, as well as being classified as an excellent hydric source. Ipalán is a depressed area, which was used for subsistence farming. It has three towns: Seima, Ayamosna and Vegaipala. The Benchigua basin has hamlets which are undergoing progressive depopulation, And lastly, Tecina-Santiago, where the second largest economic and demographic area is situated (Laguna de Santiago).

Because of this, the capital is more densely populated and the hamlets are in a state of abandonment. This has led to the land being abandoned and the people working in other sectors, such as construction, services or public administration. The San Sebastián bay has always been important due to its perfect sailing conditions, and in 1992 was the departure point of the Great

View of San Sebastián
◄ *de la Gomera.*

Part of San Sebastián de la Gomera.

Boat Race, commemorating the V Centenary; two hundred sailing boats set sail here towards America. It was the first port that Christopher Columbus arrived at on his voyage to discover the New World. It is also an area that was full of pirates such as John Hawkins, Drake or Raleigh and fuel for the flames created by others, such as Capdeville and Van der Does. But the bravery of the Gomerans never allowed these men victory, and in honour of this, which was attributed to the islanders, the chapel of Pilar was built in the church of the Asunción. The nobles régime prevented commercial development, because of

25

San Sebastián de la Gomera port.

the high taxes imposed and it was relegated to the position of administrative capital. Its isolation has also been a reason for the lack of development. The population has settled on the left side of the bay and climbs up the side of the mountain culminating on the hill of Las Nieves, where the National Parador (State owned hotel) stands, an important hotel center on the island. The old part of the city is combined with modern buildings, built on what used to be an excellent agricultural area, where

tomatoes were grown. The capital of straight roads that lead to the sea, the port is where the ferry and jet foil "Barracuda", that carry both natives and foreignors, dock. From the dock to Avalo beach you can see the Nautical Club, Lighthouse..., until you reach Punta Llana, where the sanctuary of Our Lady of Guadalupe, patron saint of La Gomera, built in the old XVI century hermitage, is situated. From the port, strolling along Fred Olsen Promenade, there is a wonderful view of the bay, and on the top of the mountain you can see the National Parador, Conde de La Gomera and the observation point of La Hila. Further along stand the Town Hall, the Government Local Office, plaza (square) de America, or Avenue of the Discoverers, which are adorned with numerous palm trees... From the top of Medio Street, you can see the Casa de la Aguada, with its well, former residence of the Counts and where Columbus obtained provisions for his three ships on his voyage that culminated in the discovery of America. After this you will find the Cabildo Insular (organization of representatives from all the towns of the islands), the parrish church of Nuestra Señora de la Asunción, la Casa

Two views of San Sebastián de la Gomera's port.

The coast of San Sebastián de la Gomera.

de Colon (Columbus' House) and the chapel of San Sebastián. At the crossroads of the "callejón" (alley) de San Sebastián, on Ruiz de Padrón road, is where the city's financial and commercial activity is located. Walking down the street, towards America or Descubridores square, there are both old and modern buildings. The "Torre del Conde" (Count's Tower) guarded by the Navy Military Headquarters, rises up on the right hand side of this street, at the end. The building of an auditorium has been planned, and it will eventually stand behind this historical monument.

Taking up the history again, la Villa was home to important conquerors until it became the dominion of the Peraza's and Herrera's. It was an important port. It had two or three towers of defense, a Dominican convent and a three naved church. In the XVIII century, its population was of almost 1 500, with a Town Hall presided over by a Mayor and his councillors. Military duties were presided over by a capitan who had the rank of commander. The men in all of these high commands were appointed by the Count.

Art on Columbina Island commenced with the Gothic period. An outstanding example of this genre, is a military monument: la Torre del Conde (the Count's tower), in the shape of a prism, with sturdy walls. The series of arches, lintels, arrow slits and ashlars of its four corners are made of red hewn stone. The building is made of stone and lime.

Regarding the religious monuments, the hermitage of San Sebastián is said to be the first temple the island ever had. Its high chapel has interesting capitals. The statue of the saint after which it is named is made of polychromed wood. There is also a statue of the Immaculate Conception which is of American origin. Another noteworthy church is that of the Asunción, on which, according to the chronicles, building started in 1502. The primitive temple had only one nave, to which others were attached together with chapels, and was finished off with XVIII porticos. The central nave was built of red hewn stone. Inside, the paving is made of stone, with wooden beams, and the places used to house the tombs are in a separate area.

The Hermigua valley. ▶

Valuable objects include the Baroque grill of the choir stalls carved out of wood, the altarpiece of the Pilar chapel, with its Mudejar coffered ceiling, a Baroque carving from the Seville School, which represents its namesake, a terracotta Saint Michael, statue of Christ crucified by José Luján Pérez, statue of the Immaculate Conception, possibly by Estévez, and by the same gentleman, a statue of Saint Peter and another of Saint Joseph. As a result of the subsequent contact between this island and the New World, due either to emigration or the arrival of people from South American countries, an unbounded interest in anything related to Latin America is born, with the creation of various institutions such as the Institute of Columbus Studies, Venezuelan Institute of Canarian Culture or the Canarian-Argentinian Cultural Centre.

After this journey through la Villa, let us look at another municipality. Drive along the north road (TF-711), leaving behind the urban centre and the districts that are surrounded by the feeling of calm exuded by banana and fruit trees, the greenhouses filled with flowers, in places that form part of San Sebastián de La Gomera: El Atajo, Ayamosna, Barranco de Santiago, Benchijigua, El Cabrito, Chejelipes, Inchereda, Jerduñe, El Jorado, Laguna de Santiago, La Laja, Lo del Gato, Lomito Fragoso and Honduras, El Molinito, San Antonio and Pilar, Seima, Tejiade, Las Toscas and Vegaipala.

Hermigua.

La Hermigua
Going up the road and after such places as El Molinito, Jaragán, Inchereda.., you will arrive at La Cumbre (the peak) tunnel, located in an area known as El Cedro (cedars), finally reaching Hermigua, along the windy road passing through Monteforte, Acebiños, Las Poyatas... Hermigua has a surface area of 39,67 km^2 and a population of 2 724. This municipality is situated to the north-east of the island, in the valley after which it is named, which is where all the activity is centered. It has been formed in the convergence of various

The outskirts of Hermigua.

ravines. At its low point, the water flow is quite strong, creating perfect conditions for irrigation farming, with banana trees forming the main crop. This has led to it being the principal area of production of this fruit on the island. The edges of the capital are practically uninhabited; as is the case of El Cedro and Los Acebiños, or the region of Montero and Taguluche, the latter due to the arid, rugged terrain. This municipality was originally the old canton of Mulaga, in the primitive period.

It is mostly an agricultural region, and half of its inhabitants work in this sector. Population growth until the end of the XIX century was slow. Lately it has increased thanks to the irrigated areas, that need labourers for the crops, and which has, for the time being, meant that emigration has been avoided. From 1 700 inhabitants in 1860, it increased to 2 800 in 1900 and to 5 800 forty years later. But the desire to head off to new horizons, to work to increase the standard of living, has gnawed at the very soul of these people and still shows in the waves of emigration.

The ravine of Hermigua originates from two small ones that converge: El Rejo and La Carbonera.

The main road from the north is the towns main road; this is where the roads and tracks that connect the various outlying districts leave from. All the commercial, administrative and religous activities of this town are concentrated along the main road. The Valle Alto (High Valley) contains districts such as El Cabo, El Convento or Lomo de San Pedro, the original areas which made up the town of Hermigua... Other places, although further away are, Monforte, El Cedro, El Cedro, El Estanquillo... El Corralete, La Cerca and Las Cabezadas. Las Hoyetas was where the first school was built. Thanks to the numerous springs, these places contain palm tree plantations which give shade to the yam trees, maize, banana trees and potatoes.. All is enveloped in mist, breeze and rain, which constantly caress the ochre green and emerald brown tones of the fertile earth.

Descending from these peaks you will arrive at the Valle Bajo (Low Valley), with a series of districts that include El Curato, Ibo-Alfaro, Piedra Romana, Palmarejo and La Castellana.. Callejón de Ordáiz. Lands protected by the winds by vines and banana trees. However, in Hermigua's geography, important dams and reservoirs have also been built, such as the one located in the Liria ravine and the one at Mulagua.

Two hamlets are tucked away in the peaks of this municipality: Los Acebiños and El Cedro, surrounded by the forrests. In the past, it was important grazing land for numerous cattle. After much work on the area, fruit trees have been planted, owned by the Cabildo Insular, and a recreation camp has been built.

The area of Montoro-Taguluche contains the districts of the same names, including El Palmar and La Caleta. This also used to be an important cattle rearing area. The ownership of small plots of land is quite common, for most of the farmable lands are owned by various important families, commonly known as caciques (derogatory term meaning local boss). The main road, that is connected to other municipalities, is home to the town's most diverse activities, with the Town Hall, the Casino, the parrish church of Santo Domingo de Guzmán, an old convent dedicated to Saint Peter, the Martyr, belonging to the Domincan Order. After the first disentailment, it became State property and was later made into the parish church. Inside there are various works of art, such as some Barroque altarpieces, a Mudejar coffered ceiling, grills of Christ and Saint Lucy, by the popular school of art and a painting of the Virgen of Candelaria. A bit further away you will find the church of La Encarnacion (Incarnation), with a wooden statue and a painting of the Virgen by Fernando Estévez.

Let's not forget the Ethnographic Museum, the most important one on the island, created by the prominant man, the best expert on Isla Colombina: Virgilio Brito.

There are also some looms, well preserved by Mistress Maruca and wooden crafts, with drums, bags... made in El Cedro.

The richness of the musical folklore has been preserved thanks to Lilí Ascanio. But when talking about Hermigua we must also mention the sea, with the rugged coastline in Santa Catalina, and beach of the same name, or the beach of La Caleta, where the salt filled sea breeze covers the brown rocks... Other places in this town are: Tabaibal, Las Poyatas, Las Nuevitas, Llano de Camo, Las Casas.

Agulo

Going back up the main road, following the bends, some 3 km from Hermigua you will come to another municipality: Agulo. It has a surface area of 25,39 km^2 and 1 464 inhabitants. The capital stands on a sort of step (balcony) which circles a rocky chain the shape of a semicircunference. Consequently there are two sectors: the lower half of Agulo and Lepe, and the upper area of Sobreagulo and Las Rosas.

It is also an area that is ideal for banana cultivation.

There are two hydric basins in Agulo where both the population and agriculture is based: the ravine of Sobreagulo, with the hamlet of La Palmita, and the ravine of Las Rosas, with the district of the same name.

Two views of Agulo.

Emigration has affected the inhabitants, but this has meant prosperity for those who have managed to make some sort of fortune in America. It is the only northern town that is not concentrated in a ravine's basin. The houses are grouped together, and the façade and appearance of many of them are architecturally beautiful, for they were once the homes of the upper classes and rich emigrants.

Agulo does not have a large population, however it is the

33

A ravine in Agulo.

municipality with the greatest number of people working on the land. Vineyards form part of the economy, and on the outskirts, there are cereal, vegetable and potato plantations. Yams are grown in the wetter areas. Fishing, the making of typical sweets and forrest farming, are other economic resources.

Its orography makes access to some areas difficult. It has the largest dam on the island, called Amalahuigue, situated in the area of Las Rosas. But Agulo is seafaring, dark skinned, as is reflected by its sand. The district of Lepe is situated on the coast, and is only accesible through the beach of Mermigua. During the fiestas (festivities) held in Agulo, marking the feast of San Juan (St. John), neibhours from various districts get together reciting satirical or comic verses and during the festivities of San Marcos (St. Mark), bonfires are lit, which the people then jump over whilst making a wish...

This municipality is popularly known as "the pearl of La Gomera" and was a place of inspiration for an eminant painter born in Cuba, José Aguiar. It was founded in 1607 by Ana de Monteverde, who brought families here from Buenavista, in the north of Nivaria. Agulo and its ravine, which lives and breaths the rough sea, enveloping the mountain of Meriga. The exotic part of Laja del Infierno, which flows into the ravine of Las Rosas. La Palmita with its hermitage dedicated to San Isidro surrounded by heather and laurisilva, and showing off its wooden craftmaking, where bags and drums are made, as in the neighbouring town of Hermigua. The temple of San Marcos, with a statue of the Virgen of Mercy...

Gastronomically speaking the dishes are rich and varied: special types of bread, curd tarts, watercress stew, marinated pork, stewed yams, almogrotes. sugar-cane juice, or gomerón...

Agula has a Friendship Centre, where people spend their spare time in the tranquility of the evenings...

Vallehermoso

And from this Gomeran balcony that harbours an infinity of desires and hopes, mirador of the Teide's silhouette, we continue our trip to another municipality, firstly upwards, then downwards along the winding road surrounded by the rugged mountain, by places such as Las Rosas, the peak of the Cepo, Lomo del Palmarejo, the ravine of Zarzales, until you can see a valley that proudly bears a stone monolith: Roque Cano. You are now in lands that belonged to the old

Vallehermoso beach.

Agana canton: Vallehermoso. At 109,31 km^2, it is the largest municipality on the island, which it crosses from north to south from Los Organos to La Rajita. Its population is of some 3 385 inhabitants. Its size is due to the appropriation in 1812, of a large part of the parrish of Chipude, when it was made into municipalities. Its main regions are: Tamargada, Agana, Vallehermoso, Chipude, Erques and Las Lomadas in the southeast, in particular La Dama. We can say that Vallehermoso lives off agriculture: bananas, potatoes, tomatoes, vineyards, palm tree honey... and Social Security pensions, as a great

A view of Vallehermoso.

number of elderly people live here. As has ocurred in other municipalities, emigration has also made an appearance here. Another important resource is fishing, above all in La Rajita. The town's activities are concentrated on two roads, on which others converge, streching out on the uneven surface. A land of steep slopes, combined with palm trees, and various types of laurisilva.
Vallehermoso is situated between the ravines of Ingenio and Macayo. Traditional and modern architecture stand hand in hand, painted in white, and its parish in honour of St. John the Baptist, dates back to 1632. It was a prosperous district in days gone by, thanks to commerce, agriculture and cattle rearing, but drought together with bad political management and the prohibition of grazing animals on the land, decimated its economy. However, in spite of these ups and downs, it is considered a district with a strong social movement. The Agricultural Co-operative of Vallehermoso was created in 1986, that has a large number of

Valle Gran Rey. ▶

farmers, to help overcome the crisis endured by the municipality.

Other areas co-exist within the large territorial spectrum of Vallehermoso, such as the hamlet of Tamargada, which has maintained its country traditions intact; it has a hermitage in honour of the Virgen of Charity. Epina and its famous streams. The peak of Chigueré with its sheer drop to the sea where nature sculpted one of its works of art: Los Organos. Sepultura beach, the centre of Arguamul, with the moutain of Teselinde wathcing over the hermitage of Santa Clara. The Alojera coast, the cliffs of Tejeleche... Tazo, the first sanctuary on the islnd dedicated to St. Lucy. Chipude or Temocodá, prominant for its popular culture and ancestral folklore, situated in the old canton of Orone. A place of emigration in a majestic natural headland: La Fortaleza (The Fortress). Traditional surroundings in the making of original pottery, in El Cercado. Its church, houses various monstrances that date back

to the XVII and XVIII centuries. Vallehermoso and its famous festivities in honour of the Virgen del Carmen. A land which, in spite of its changing circumstances, looks to progress. Other districts and hamlets: Alojera, Banda de Las Rosas, Los Bellos, Chapines, La Dehesa, Erquito, Igualero, Los Loros, Macayo, Pavón, La Quilla, Rosa de las Piedras, Valle Abajo.

Valle Gran Rey

Continuing along the winding road built in El Palmar, head towards a municipality located further down, until you come to a beautiful shelf, which housed the first Town Hall: Arure. If you look at the view from here you will spot, with great vertigo, the existing ravine. In its bed... Valle Gran Rey. It has a surface area of 32,36 km^2 and a population of 2968. It is the most westerly municipality on the island and slightly larger than Agulo. It contains three prominant areas: the basin of Arure, Taguluche and the actual municipal capital, where the

Valle Gran Rey.

Arure.

majority of the population lives.

The Valle Gran Rey ravine, was an area of great tradition amongst the pre-hispanic population, as the nucleus of the so called Orone, place of residence of the great indigenous kings such as Unichepe. After the conquest, the first counts of Gomera chose this as one of their places of residence. Until 1930, Arure was the municipal city, after which Calera took over, when the coast began to be put to commercial use and the irrigated land was found to be perfect for the tasks involved. Arure was the oldest capital on the island with a church dedicated to Our Lady of Health. Arure and its Risco (cliff) de Heredia and Farfán Mountain. Arure and its sheep and goat rearing. Arure, and its pastrymaking, with its curd tarts. One of Valle Gran Rey's main resources is centered around agriculture, in the shape of banana cultivation, as there is an abundance of springs and wells. This is followed by fishing, in the sea faring district of Las Vueltas, one of the most important on the island. The services sector comes next, and to a lesser extent, tourism, due to the excellent climate.

The majority of day to day activities are centered around the main road and side roads that lead to the beach: La Calera, Borbalán, Las Vueltas...

Other places worth mentioning also form part of Valle Gran Rey; the observation point of el Santo (the Saint), by St. Mary's hermitage; the hillside of Taguluche and its white hamlet, that descends into Guariñen

beach. Las Hayas, on the flatland, which has the constant blessing of the Virgen de Coromoto, Patron Saint of Venezuela. Palmarejo and its hermitage to San Antonio... The devout Valle Gran Rey, lands of faith... the Hermitage of la Virgen del Buen Paso. Valle Gran Rey, with its yam orchards, sugar-cane plantations and palm trees. Valle Gran Rey, with its handicrafts, where bags, drums, and farming tools are made...

And Valle Gran Rey immersed in history, for it is said that the inhabitants bought these lands from the Count, thanks to some treasure left by pirates in Inglés beach. After the emancipation from the nobles and thanks to hydric wealth, the Comunidades de Regantes (an association created to regulate the watering of the land) was created. The Count and Countess' pools, where the nobles of the island used to bathe...

The chronicles also report that the hill of la Baja del Secreto, was where the men who assasinated Fernán Peraza met.

Other places: Casa de la Seda (Silk House), Los Granados, El Guro, Hornillo, Lomo del Balo, La Pintilla, Retamal, Los Reyes, La Vizcaína.

On from the beach, lashed by the fiery, yet somehow quiet sea, continue along the main road once more until you come to another municipality, the sixth and last of those that make up the island. Uphill, passing through Arure with its wonderful fertile valley and towards Las Hayas, you will come to a crossroads that will lead you into the

National Park of Garajonay, to then descend until you can see the first hamlets of this new municipal territory: Imada. Further south, you will stumble across the capital, after which the municipality is named, and which we will now look at: Alajeró.

Alajeró

Alajeró has a surface area of 49,42 km^2 and a population of some 1 415 inhabitants. It is the most depressed municipality in La Gomera. Its relief is

Fields in Alajeró.

one of the less rugged. It is full of ravines, such as Santiago and Guarimiar. Apart from the area around the peak, the rest has very little humidity.

As has occured in the other municipalities, agriculture has been one of its sources of income, with bananas, tomatoes..., and also fishing. Part of its population works in construction and services. There has been a tourism boom around Santiago beach. Its hermitage was set alight here by Dutch pirates in 1599.

Alajeró stands between the cantons of Orone and Ipalán. Alajeró and its

Santiago Beach.

Santiago Beach. Hermitage of the Virgen.

economy. Alajeró, an orchard with orange trees, coffee, mango and avocado plantations. Lands of faith and devotion, testified by the different religious buildings: temple of San Salvador, hermitage of San Lorenzo (the second oldest after St. Lucy of Tazo, in the Lomo de Arabguerode), hermitage of San Isidro, on El Calvario Mountain, of Our Lady of el Buen Paso, Patron Saint of Alajeró, whose festivity is celebrated in September.
Alajeró and its hamlets which are almost jam packed together, all the way down from the peak to the coast: Arguayoda, Quise, Antoncojo,

The port at Santiago Beach.

church, which contains a wooden statue of Christ. Alajeró is like the small municipal capital of the whole archipelago.
Herds of goats used for milking, and from which wonderful cheeses are made, graze around the northern town of Imada. Loma de Arguayoda, Roques de Imada, del Becerro, del Calvario; the hillside of Artamache and terraces of Tajonaje, the ravines of Quise and Erese... Alajeró, the island's granary, was important within the islands

Guarimiar, Los Almácigos, Targa....
Alajeró looking to new horizons, to
new cultures that it protects along its
hospitable coast..
Along the road that crosses the district of
Tecina, on Santiago beach, go uphill to
get on to the road that will take you once
more to San Sebastián, where our
journey ends. Along the way you will see
mountains, ravines, hillsides, all cloaked
in silence. Around the area of la Villa, you
will see Las Toscas, Destene Mountain,
the observation point of Vegaipala,
before connecting up with the road that
will take you to the island's capital. Along
this route, you can still admire the
untamed, almost virgen landscape: Juan
de Vera Ravine, Tagamiche, Ayamosma,
Loma del Camello.
The coastline of San Sebastián de La
Gomera, a bay with thousands of houses:
a sea dotted with an infinite number of
boats, on their way to other locations.

Garajonay National Park
Because of its great interest, I wanted
to include Garajonay National Park as a
separate chapter.
The National Park of Garajonay is
situated in the central plateau and
includes the largest area of forrests,
extending for some 3 948 hectares. It is
the pinnacle of the six municipalities
that make up Junonia Menor. Its
highest point is called the Pico (the
Peak), with a height of 1 487 m.
Regarding its geological aspect, we can
say that it is almost entirely made up of
basaltic materials. Due to the effects of
the volcanoes, many hills were formed,

View of the Garajonay National Park

giving it a majestic air. A few of the
most impressive ones are Chejelipín
Hill, which is 1 364 m high, and on its
edge those of Agando, Ojila and La
Zarcita. The most striking of these
three is 1 251m high. The Benchijigua
ravine to the south and La Laja ravine
to the east separate this rocky mass.
The trade winds play an important role
in the increase of humidity, which has
meant that the abundant vegetation is
perennial. It is an area of almost
constant rainfall. There are four types
of vegetation: laurisilva, of which there
are believed to be about eighteen
species, fayal-brezal (similar to
heather), pine forrest and cactus. This
vegetation comprises some important
forrest areas such as Meriga, Los
Acebiños, El Cedro, Ancón del
Pajarito... Apart from the
aforementioned plant life, other
vegetation shares this habitat. There
are also the sabinas, or rare types of
plants such as the everlasting flowers,
the Epina tree, the Magaña dragon tree

and cedars of Agando. Regarding the fauna, this is largely made up of rabbits, rats, bats, wild cats, rabiche doves, wild canaries, chaffinches... There has been constant contact with man, for it provided him with land for ploughing, pasture for the cattle, wood and coal mines. However, after it was declared an area of National Interest, according to the Law of 25th March, 1981, these activities stopped, and it became a place to be enjoyed by everyone.

Laguna Grande (Big Lagoon), is a place of public interest, within this area, with its hermitage dedicated to the Virgen of Lourdes, where each year the most deep rooted festivities on the island are held, known as the festivities of El Cedro, as occurs in Merigo. Various roads and tracks surround the Park, one of the most important being the one that links San Sebastián to Valle Gran Rey.

A forrest of "laurisilva" (wet forrest) in Garajonay National Park.

EL HIERRO

ESCALA 1:180.00

EL GOLFO

ATLÁNTICO

OCÉANO

El Julán

Bahía de las Calcosas

Roques de las Palomas

Punta del Machuco

Pta. del Norte

Riscos de los Cardones

Punta de Amacas

Playa del Salto

Playas Largas

Pta. de la Caleta

Playa de la Caleta

Aeropuerto de El Hierro

Valverde

Tamaduste

Ermita de San Lázaro

Echedo

Hoyo

Refenama

Monacal

Tesbabo

Erese

Pozo de las Calcosas

Bahía del Negro

La Pepelera

Pta. de Agache

Roque de Salmor

Pto. de la Estaca

Pta. de Tijimiraque

S. Telmo

San Telmo

Pta. de Ajones

Pta. de la Bonanza

540

MONTAÑA LADERA

CHAMUSCADA 1136

Tiñor

Las Montañetas

Las Rosas

La Torre

Los Llanos

Isora

Tajace

S. Andrés

Los Mocanes

Frontera

Las Casas

Taibique

El Río

Los Jables

Playa de Arena

Las Playas

Playa Calcosas

Pta. de Miguel

Bahía de Miguel

Playa Brava

Playa del Cantadal

Pta. del Miradero

Roques de los Joraditos

RESTINGA 197

La Restinga

Punta Restinga

Punta del Lance

El Lajial

Bahía de Naos

Punta de los Frailes

Roque de Naos

Cueva del Gaterón

Playa de Lines

Punta Lajas del Lance

El Río

Punta de Telera

Virgen de la Peña

Guarazoca

Jarales

Las Puntas

Ermita de la Caridad

Embarcadero de Punta Grande

Punta Negra

Playa de Punta Grande

Playa los Corrales

Bahía de los Pozos

Roques de la Sal

Bahía del Hoya

Playa de la Tabla

Pta. de los Palos

Casas Guinea

Los Llanillos

Tigaday

Las Toscas

Ladera Cabello

TENERIFE 1.416

MERCADAL 1.253

Cruz de los Reyes

MALPASO 1.500

Cruz de los Humilladeros 1216

VENTEJEA

El Sabinar

Pozo de la Salud

Sabinosa

Valle Quemado

Santuario de Ntra. Sra. de los Reyes

La Dehesa

TENACA 624

TABAIBAL

406

Faro de Orchilla

Pta. Vejeras

Pta. de Arenas Blancas

Pta. Tosca Arnariia

Roque de la Sal

Pta. del Verodal

Bahía de los Reyes

Pta. de la Dehesa

Pta. de los Reyes

Playa de la Madera

Punta del Barouqo

Punta de la Palometa

Pozo de los Mozos

Punta de la Pajera

EL HIERRO

Geography

El Hierro and La Palma are the youngest islands in the archipelago. El Hierro has a surface area of 268,70 km², making it the smallest island in the Canaries, and the one located furthest west and south. It is situated between lattitudes 27° 38' and 27° 51' N and longitudes 17° 53' and 18° 09' E of the Greenwich Meridian. Its small surface area, together with its greater altitude, make it on average, the island with the steepest slopes. It is triangular shaped, and the following places are situated at each angular point: to the northeast, Punta del Guanche; to the south, Punta Restinga; and to the west, Punta Orchilla.

Its high slopes together with its geological formation, indicate the difficulty in building sheltered harbours. Its coastline is practically all cliffs, with two sandy beaches: La Restinga and Las Playas.

The most important geographical accident is El Golfo, semicircular in shape, with slopes of up to 1 200m high. The cliffs of this sort of crater, are, at some points, more than 1 100 m high (Fuga de Gorreta). Due to succesive geological modifications, the foot of El Golfo is almost flat, and occupies an area of close to 20 km². Some important hydric deposits have been found.

The area of El Julán is a large hillside with incredible escarpments at some points, and the surface is indented with

The land and sea of the island of El Hierro.

various ravines which lead off to the south. La Dehesa is situated in the upper area and has a deep rooted cattle rearing tradition. It runs into Punta de Orchilla in the southeast, the most westerly point of the archipelago, which was considered the Zero Meridian. Along its eastern coast the semicircular shaped slopes lined up one after the other, leave the ground very uneven and the materials it is composed of have formed into an immense beach, commonly known as Las Playas (The Beaches).

As it was formed relatively recently, and

45

A sea of lava in La Restinga.

due to the small amount of erosion because the terrain has hardly evolved at all, you will come accross another wonderful landscape: the Nisdafe Plateau. The soil here may be the product of what was previously a forrest area, but today it is used as pasture, the growing of fodder and cereals. It occupies an area of approximately 50 km². The average height is of 900 m, and there are various volcanic cones nearby. Other topographic phenomenon worth

View of El Golfo from the observation
◀ *point at la Peña*

mentioning, are the collection of Roque de la Sal, to the west and the Roques de Salmor, to the northeast. Malpaso is the highest peak, standing 1 500 m high; followed by Tenerife at 1 416 m and Tabano at 1 387 m.

Climate
It has always been considered a dry island, the problem probably consisting in, firstly the porosity of the ground, which absorbs rainfall, and secondly, the lack of impermeable ground. The climatic conditions of El Hierro are very

Prickly Pear in Taibique.

Aeonium.

similar to the other western islands. The altitude of the slopes of El Golfo and the island's location with regard to the trade winds, mean that a large area does obtain moisture. This area extends from El Golfo, through Nisdafe (El Fayal) to Valverde.

El Hierro's position within the archipelago, makes it the most oceanic and the one furthest from Africa, and is therefore more able to receive the impact of the Atlantic's wet storms. Its southerly location means it is the one closest to the arid, tropical area. If we take these circumstances into account and include its orography, we could say that its climate is similar to the islands of Fuerteventura and Lanzarote, with windward and leeward climatic stratum. Its morphology and above all the area of El Golfo, makes it an area which suffers many storms. This was mentioned by the XIX century statistician Escolar y Serrano, who wrote: "The diverse climate and the effects of the heat and cold are greater than those in the concave, in the convex part of the island. The terrain, with steep slopes, does not only lack forrests and springs, but is also exposed, at the end of the summer and most of autumn, to the scorching heat of the east winds, and in winter to the violent fury of the storms. The latter ravage the concave part of the island, because of its position and the lie of the land, more than the convex part. The wind blows freely and without opposition through this area, whilst in the concave area, its encounter with the mountains greatly increases the violent nature of its whirlwinds, which blow down trees, tear the tiles off rooves, and cause immense damage to the vineyards and other plantations".

Hydrology

As we already mentioned in the section on geography and climate, the almost complete absence of springs makes this island dry. But this dryness stems from the fact that it is a young island, the soil being composed of substances that come from recent lava fall, which is very porous and absorbs rainfall. The tiny population and lack of means available, have practically stopped the excavation of subterranean wells, although drilling has started again quite recently.

Vegetation

The way the vegetation is distributed is conditioned by moisture and temperature. The wetter areas are found in the north and northeast, with the same type of plants, for grazing somewhat reduced the evolution of the vegetation. Vegetation can be divided into four types. The first corresponds to the basal or coast, up to approximately 300 m in the north and 500 m in the south. Slight rainfall and the powerful effects of the sun, have led to the existence of xerophilous plants such as the tabaiba, incense or jirdama and salado or calcosa The balo and cardon (type of giant cactus) are not very common. The reason they still grow is because the land that sustains them is no good for cattle raising or agricultural use. Two examples are Punta de Orchilla and El Lajial. Over 300 m and up to 600 m, you come

Agave in the hills of Salmor.

Observation point in la Peña.

into the sabinar area, which is resistent to drought. It is accompanied by a few dragon trees or palmtrees. The area which contains the greatest number of these is in La Dehesa.

El Julán's sabinares, in harmony with Sabinosa's pine forrests... The best examples in the whole archipelago are found in El Hierro.

The wind's impact has forced many sabinas to adopt the direction it blows in and their roots, many of them centuries old, are spread out on the ground.

At 600m to 1 200 m, you enter into the area of monteverde. A clear exponent of this was in Nisdafe until the XVII century, when the lands were ploughed, leaving only the area of El Fayal. The Cuesta de Jinama also forms part of this area.

Fayal-brezal is common here, withstanding the heat and drought with no apparant effort, more resistant than the laurisilva.

However, apart from the aforementioned vegetation, the Garoé or Holy Tree, was also a legend amongst the bimbaches (a tribe). Of the laurisilva family, a linden to be more specific, it had luxuriant foliage and a great capacity for distillation, due to the moisture brought by the winds. It was located in the Los Lomos area and supplied the villagers here, but was destroyed by a strong storm in the year 1610. Sinonymous with this, there is a sabina in the Cruz de los Reyes area which has a similar use.

The woods lie amid constant

A forrest of "laurisilva".

tranquitility, such as the Canarian pine tree, that grows in the centre and south of the island. It needs little moisture, but plenty of heat, and is fire resistant in the event of a forrest fire, as it grows back effortlessly. The principal pine tree populations are found in El Salvador and Los Reyes, occupying some 500 hectares. You can also spot pine trees that have been brought from North America, in particular from Canada, in harmony with the existing fayal-brezal. Pine forrests that lend shade to the thyme and tolerate its existence on its edges...

50

Economy

El Hierro's economy has been based mainly on agriculture and cattle rearing. Agriculture has brought in more income in the municipality of Frontera, than in Valverde, as it has spread out into the service sector, creating jobs in commerce, transport, construction and industry.

El Hierro has always exported a great deal of its produce, such as orchilla (a type of lichen), hierba pastel (a plant) and vines. Cattle exports also had their heyday a few decades ago. The decrease in agriculture has been due to various factors, these include the lack of water in the lower areas that is needed for irrigation farming and its isolation at sea, due to the fact that it has no good port, as its coastline offers no natural shelter. The current dock, equipped as best as possible, and with the proper technology (La Estaca), does not satisfy demand or needs, because, as occured in other ports, when bad weather takes hold, it is impossible to load or unload goods. Another important dock was Puerto Naos, in La Restinga. Its fitting-out and the way it was classified as the port of the old dock of La Estaca, was due to the previous Spanish Chief of State: Francisco Franco Bahamonde, who created a Plan de Adopción (Adoption Plan) for those areas with bad communications, in order to improve them. Said plan was approved in 1960 but did not come into effect until ten years later. In those years, the roads of El Hierro were not tarmacked. The airport was built in 1972, in the area of el Llano del Cangrejo, which was another great help for the economy.

The importance of agriculture has been based on subsistance farming products, such as wheat, barley, rye, and to a lesser extent, millet; these are followed by pod vegetables, potatoes, vines and fruit, in particular figs.

Disentailment in the XIX century, brought with it the demarcation of the land, some being alloted to agricultural use and other areas to cattle rearing, and for this purpose stone walls were built. Cattle rearing has also contributed to the improvement of the economy. The distribution carried out confirms this, and is the reason why there is such an abundance of livestock, with sheep in the hamlets of San Andrés and El Pinar; goats in Isora, El Pinar and La Dehesa; and bovine cattle in El Mocanal, Guarazoca and San Andrés. Apart from meat production, cheese, which is of very good quality, is another important product.

Going back to agriculture, banana cultivation has decreased lately, and has been substitued by tropical pinappple, which is both very popular and lucrative.

Demography

Its size and orography have made El Hierro the least populated island of the archipelago. The is due to the shortage of water and lack of natural shelters along its coastline, and makes the development of a fishing industry, which would enhance the economy, unforseeable. The population has therefore settled in the centre and in particular, around the wetter areas. Consequently, the capital Valverde, is the only one in the Canary Islands that is not situated by the sea.

The population has occupied a large part of the Nisdafe plateau, scattered around the north and northeast up to Valverde. In the south, the population goes through Azofa and up to El Pinar. The opposite occurs in El Julán and La Dehesa, areas that have remained preactically uninhabited, due to the arid, rugged terrain, in the former, and because the land has been given over to communal pasture in the latter. In previous times, the Valle del Golfo, was an unimportant area, due to the aridity and its unsuitability for subsistance farming, because the aquiferous wells had not been tapped. From its colonization to the first half of this century, the number of inhabitants increased, until, in 1940, they amounted to more than 9 500. However, emigration made an impression on the population, and it decreased, as a result of the search for a better life in Latin America and in the provincial capitals of the Canary Islands: Santa Cruz de Tenerife and Las Palmas de Gran Canaria. At present, the largest settlements are in Valverde, Frontera, Tigaday, Taibique and el Mocanal, also increasing in El Golfo because of the growth of exports.

Crafts

Garoé or Meridiano island, has the most textile mills, transforming the raw material into knapsacks, rucksacks, bags, handbags, etc. They are made in Mocanal, Guarazoca, Erese, Taibique, Isora, San Andrés, Las Casas and Sabinosa.

In the making of percussion instruments, Taibique and Guarazoca are the most important, the latter also making escobón (type of tree). mulberry or granadillo castanets, and large, cilinder shaped drums made of leather. In Frontera whistles are crafted,

El Hierro's crafts.

made from both wood and metal. Wooden crafts are found in San Andrés and Mocanal, around Taibique... In Sabinosa you will find tin crafts, in the shape of lanterns, milk churns or oil lamps.

Le Hero is an island with a profuse wickerwork tradition, using sabina as the raw material. Wickerwork from Sabinosa, El Pinar... Taibique with its straw wickerwork, and as the eminent ethnologist and folklorist Manuel Pérez Rodriguez states:

Sabinosa: the craftsman Juan Pérez Hernández.

Wickerwork from Sabinosa.

"especially the taños, used to store grain; the paciles used to store dried figs and the foras to keep the gofio (thick flour made from maize, corn or barley)"
Craftsmen who work in peaceful surroundings on an island that is breaking into everlasting progress...

Folklore
The island of El Hierro has also held onto its oldest customs and traditions. Sabinosa with its "Baile del Vivo" (Dance of the Living), the Flaire in Taibique, Tajanara to the tune of the bucio, where the youngsters, hand out

a dead animal at night, to those people who have behaved badly within the community.
El Hierro with its lobas or poems dedicated to the Virgen, both holy and profane. Its romances which show the knowledge and the history of this people that have been neglected for so long.
Other dances practised in this Atlantic Hesperides are: El Santo (the Saint), the Tango, el Conde de Cabra (the Count of Cabra), de la Virgen (the Virgen)...
And songs such as the arrorró, the meda (with Berber connotations), songs when at work: ploughing,

53

Typical house in El Hierro.

reaping, grinding, collecting figs, cutting leaves, etc. Both songs and dances are accompanied by instruments, typical of this area: chácaras, whistles and drums. The more recent folklore includes, Cuban songs and dances and bailes de cuerda. A prestigous investigator, Manuel J. Lorenzo Perera speaks of these: "The so called bailes de cuerda (literally, string dances) are closely related to two historical events, which, at the same time, overlap: the progressive arrival on the island of the "indianos" (Spanish emigrant returned from Latin America) who came back from Cuba, and the creation of the first societies or casinos at the end of the XIX century and beginning of the XX. Little by little the presence of guittar, mandola and lute players increased, and in the recently formed societies the string dances were practised to the beat of these instruments.This concept includes a collection of dances, common even in rural areas of XVIII Europe ("Folías",

"Malagueñas", "Seguidillas", "Isas") and XIX century (Polka, Mazurka, Berlina) which arrived on Hierro, like many other things, quite late: "Candels and carbide were placed on the wall even then, when the string dances took place. In the fields, they were practised for the first time after the year 1912. In Valverde, before this". Although they were originally dances that you danced without a partner, in the open air, and with stunning coreography, in the casinos they were adapted to the new fashion of pair dancing, common practise, even in the archipelago, since the middle of the last century. All of this was linked to the aperturista movement (greater freedom), observed in El Hierro at the time, in which the "indianos" played such an important role. When it first arrived, pair dancing (the same has occured with the majority of new fashions introduced on the island), was greeted with the customary opposition. The increase of the number of societies -where dances take place almost exclusively on Sundays and feast days- has gone hand in hand with the increase in population, and in some cases, the participants had to take turns. This situation led to controversial and polemic arguments, which in more than one case was solved by the old people there simply hitting those involved.

For a few years now, mainly around the time of the fesitivities of "la Bajada de la Virgen" (Virgen's Descent), in the casinos and popular fairs held in the town squares (lately accompanied by orchestras) a small group of people, practically all of them of Venezuelan origin, return to the island, dressed in various ways, with brightly coloured shirts, and bringing with them the songs and customs of Venezuela, with dances such as the Joropo (popular dance of the Venezueland lowlanders), Guaracha (Antillean song and dance) and Bolero.

Art

Throughout history, Le Hero has possessed wonderful examples of art. Even before the conquest, artistic displays abounded. The natural environment and the inhabitants jobs, in this case, shepherds, and the habitat in which they develop, create what is necessary to achieve a more comfortable lifestyle, without stopping to think that at that moment, they are producing art. In previous times there were three types of habitat: caves-as rooms or ceremonial caves, artificial structures and concheros (place used in pre-historic times to store seafood such as shells, moluscs and fish). Taros (curvineal stone shelters) and Tágorores, larger and in the shape of a semi-circle, were some of the artificial structures, which are thought to have been used as meeting places. An example of this is the tágoror of El Julán. This place also has a famous conchero and singular inscriptions or engravings on various stones, that are very characteristic.

Pottery is almost unknown. The few fragments found, lead us to believe that it was simple and rustic. As there are practically no areas of clay (only a little in the region of Azofa), the raw materials necessary to be able to speak of a deep rooted pottery making tradition are non existent, and there are no potters in El Hierro today. Regarding the art of cave paintings, and in particular, engravings, it was discovered almost at the end of the last century by Aquilino Padrón. We can distinguish two types: alphabetic inscriptions which come from the mediterranean area and ideograms that

Tower of Our Lady of the Conception in Valverde.

55

are geometrical, circular, chequered, or shaped like a horseshoe, similar to those discovered in northwest Africa and the Sahara. They date back to the years 200 to 700 A.D.

Within the different periods of art, the Barroque style, because of its importance, left its mark on religous architecture. The churches of San Antonio Abad in El Pinar, and Nuestra Señora de Candelaria (Our Lady of Candelaria), in Frontera, which do not have bell towers, are good examples of this style. Bell gables with an exterior access can be seen in the hermitages of Nuestra Señora de la Consolación (Our Lady of Consolation), in Sabinosa, San Andrés (St. Andrew) in the hamlet named after him, Nuestra Señora de los Reyes (Our Lady of Kings), in La Dehesa, which also has battlements with a Mudejar feel to them, and the Church of Nuestra Señora de la Concepción (Our Lady of the Conception), in Valverde, which contains eighteenth-century paintings, with Barroque touches.

History

The chronicles state that the primitive Herreños were of medium build, strong, agile and brave. Their tales bordered on sadness, with pitiful tones to their songs and the dances practised were in circles. Polygamy did not exist and they were not able to marry women from their own clan. Le Hero was ruled by a goodnatured prince: Armiche, who was taken prisoner in the conquest and enslaved by Jean de Bethencourt. Their dress was similar to that of the inhabitants of Fuerteventura: a robe made from sheepskin. They used big, strong wooden staffs to help them scramble over the rocks. Their houses were circular shaped and they sheltered twenty odd people of the same clan. The caves built on the coast also had the same use.

Sabino Berthelot wrote: "Water from the reservoirs (Heres) and an opportune spring that ran at the foot of the famous Garoé, was their main drink." With the fruit picked from the mocanes tree, they made a type of

Cave paintings at El Julán.

fermented liqueur. They ate gofio (made from fine maize, flour and sugar) and roast meats (kid, lamb...). It is possible that they also ate the meat of giant lizards. But the most highly prized meat was that of fat sheep, which they called Juhaques, and which were generally eaten during the national festivities (Guatatiyoas). The Ben-Bachirs or bimbaches, also appreciated shellfish, especially limpets. Their favourite fruit was figs, which grows in great quantities on the island. From the roots of the fern Pteris aquilina, they made flour, which they ate in times of shortage. They worshiped natural phenomenon, which they considered as gods, such as Eraoranhan, Moheyra...

Regarding the island's name, there are many theories as to its origin, mostly based on mythology rather than other aspects. One of these theories points to the abundance on the island of ferruginous soil ("hierro" means iron in Spanish). In fact the French called it Fer Island.. Viera and Clavijo state "the first inhabitants of this island, aware of the enormous amounts of raw iron, called it Hierro. However, not only was this source of wealth abandoned because of the lazyness of the nobles, they in fact forgot about it completely." The pirates had already roamed around Meridiano Island, and had even made slaves of some of the inhabitants, but it was not until the time of the conquest by the Crown of Castile, when the Frenchman Jean de Bethencourt weighed anchor and commenced his

raids, overcoming the natives and taking their king and one hundred odd people prisoner, due to the treachery of Armiche's brother, Augeron. Maybe also because of the predictions of the fortune-teller Yoñe before his death. Once Bethencourt the Great, had subjected the natives, a colony of French, Flemish, and Spaniards settled on the island, patronised by him. They all abused and were corrupt with the natives, who had to suffer humiliation, insults and the rape of their wives and childresn. Bethencourt appointed Lázaro Vizcaíno as Governor, who turned a blind eye to the contained anger and protests of the Herreños, but was finally killed by a bimbache. The shrewd Maciot, wishing to be civil with the inhabitants, appointed another Governor and punished some of the soldiers implicated in the repeated atrocities with death, so that the island could be at peace once more.

Gastronomy
The cuisine of El Hierro is both curious as well as tasty. The dishes are vast and varied, and some very old recipes are still present on the dinner tables of many families. Amongst these are fern, tarangontía, gofio (made with fine maize flour and sugar) and tafeña tarts, with a variety of grain.

Their culinary art includes roast snails, black pudding, cheese escaldón de mojo and cheese and milk broth; burgado, limpet or crab soups. Chick pea, and millet flowers stew... Golden thistle, millet or radish salads. Dishes based on pod vegetables, such as kidney beans, "fricasseé" (meat stew with an egg sauce and milk), lentils... The potato, which is fundamental to the Canary Island cuisine, apart from mainly accompanying meat and fish, is also eaten on its own, in various different ways "arrugadas", stewed, with eggs and cheese, fried in breadcrumbs, or dipped in mojos: of garlic and coriander, or fried and boiled mojos, etc.

Fish dishes include peto casseroles, conejo de mar asado, jaquetas, moreys. Bird dishes: stuffed chicken, pardelas, rancho of wild pigeon. Meat dishes include: chivito with mojo made from garlic, kid, truchas de carne de cochino, ferret, small birds, fried blood, steak, fresh meat stew, etc. Stewed, or roast fish, or with mojo; roast meats, cooked in the oven with succulent salmorejos that are absolutely delicious. All these dishes are washed down with good wines, in which a lot of effort has gone into producing...

Regarding sweets and desserts, there are arropes (thick, cooked grape juice to which pieces of fruit are added), peaches in wine, dried fig cream, belete and curd, amongst others. As a liqueur, mistela (grape juice mixed with alchohol and sugar).

This isle of the Ben-Bachirs has a rich cuisine and the people, in search of a better life, took the recipes with them. But although far from their land, memories and nostalgia remained with them always. The dishes are also greatly appreciated by many visitors.

Tourism

As a whole, and in spite of its size, El Hierro offers a wide variety of things to do. Its capital Valverde, has many wonderful nooks and crannies with which you can start your tourist trail. Other points of interest are: Frontera, situated near El Golfo and full of vineyards and fruit trees. Sabinosa, with the Well of Health, famous for its medicinal waters. La Restinga, a southern port, with excellent fishing. El Tamaduste, a natural pool of cristal clear, calm waters, about 3 km away from the airport.

Tiñor, a hamlet surrounded by a forrest of laurisilva, situated between Valverde and San Andrés, at the start of the high plateau of Nisdafe. It is an area given over to grazing, where the green fields are covered in volcanic stone.

Malpaso Peak, is an excellent observation point, where you can look out onto El Golfo and the rest of the island.

Orchilla Lighthouse, in the extreme west of the island. In the past it was known as the end of the world, as it coincided with the point which the Zero Meridian passed through. During the times of Ptolomy, it passed through the Canary Islands and since the XV and XVII centuries it has officially passed through, Orchilla Point.

El Sabinar, a forrest of thousand year old sabinas, that is unique in the Canary Islands, situated on the slopes of the extreme west of the island.

El Garoé or Holy Tree, was a linden tree that grew on the northern slopes, between Tiñor and las Montañetas. The natives of El Hierro obtained their water supply thanks to this tree, for when the clouds, blown by the Trade Winds passed through its leaves, they were impregnated with water which fell to the ground. In 1610, a hurracaine destroyed this interesting tree. In 1949, at the instigation of Valverde Casino, another linden, with the same characteristics as the former one, was planted and blessed by the Carmalite father Pelayo.

Lajiales (figures formed by lava) exist in different areas on the island, the most important of which lie in the south. They are also called Lava Cordada (Chordate Lava) and are of interesting shapes.

40% of El Hierro has been declared a National Park. The largest area is located in the west, with a great variety of ecosystems: Fayal-brezal and laurisilva forrest in the high part of the island and northern slopes towards the Golfo Valley. Canarian Pine Tree, in the upper regions and eastern, southern and western slopes. Los Lajiales, with a chordate lava surface in the extreme south.

El Julán, whose slopes are made of lava and are used as grazing land, in the center of which we can see petroglyphs, that strech almost from the southern tip to near the extreme west.

La Dehesa, a communal area, used as grazing land for the cattle, situated in the western part, 400 to 800 m above sea level.

El Verodal, an area of lava and red sand beach, on the west and northwest coast.

Another important tourist area is the Golfo Valley. It can be seen from the observation point of La Peña, where there is a wonderful restaurant set up by the recently deceased Cesar Manrique, and the Jinama restaurant. It is the largest valley in the Canary Islands. The tallest point of this depression stands some 1000 m high, with sheer walls in the centre and festooned with trees and flora

Two aspects of la Peña observation point.

Sabinosa and its surrounds.

characteristic of this area. Over 14 km long, it streches from los Roques de Salmor to the observation point of El Ricón or Bascos. It embraces practically all of the northern coast. The hamlet and the rich agricultural area, which is the most important on the island is located in the bottom of the valley. This peaceful place, where you can sip its wines and taste its fish, is known as both El Golfo and La Frontera. The coastline, rugged but beautiful, has several coves where you can swim. Continuing along the edge of this valley, you will come to the hamlet of Sabinosa, a rich folkloric and handicraft area on the island. At the foot of this lies the Pozo de la Salud (Well of Health), a place of rest for all those who try out the curative properties of its water. The spa is going to be opened shortly, with a hotel which will provide all the services intrinsic to this type of facility.

The southern slope of the island is an enormous area given over to grazing land. It offers a wonderful view and its slopes are full of craters that descend giddily to the sea, popularly known as Mar de las Calmas (Sea of Calms) because of its almost motionless waters, that make it look like a huge lake. It is an excellent fishing area and a wonderful place to go to get away from it all and relax. La Restinga, a fishing village, is situated along the coast here, and its almost 400 inhabitants make their living from catching tuna and other fish. Driving up the road, you can see the famous Lajiales and you will then reach the region of El Pinar, with a characteristic Canarian Pine tree forrest, a nature park where you can camp. Continuing along this tourist route, you will eventually reach the observatory point of Las Playas (the beaches), that make up the south of the island. On one side is the Roque de Bonanza and on the other the National Parador.

In the western most part of El Hierro, La Dehesa, there are several places worth visiting: Orchilla Lighthouse, el Sabinar, and the hermitage of Our Lady of Kings, Patron Saint of the island. Other important points are: Tiñor, El Tamaduste, La Caleta, Timijiraque, Mocanal, Erese, Guarazoca...

El Hierro with simple but beautiful and interesting tourist routes, is like a dream come true.

Fauna

El Hierro's fauna, both its sea creatures as well as those animals that live on land or keep guard from the air, are very similar to those of the other islands. One of the creatures of note is the giant lizard, that lives on the enigmatic Roques (Rocks) de Salmor, hence their name.

MUNICIPALITIES

Valverde

It has a surface area of 103,64 km2 and a population of 3 590. It encompasses the northeast of the island up to El Pinar and including Las Playas. It has three large regions: Los Lomos and Nisdafe, Valverde and Los Barrios and Azofa. The most prosperous area is the Nisdafe plateau, with an altitude that ranges from 900 to 1000 m. It is greatly influenced by the Trade Winds, and is the best area, economically speaking, for both agriculture and cattle raising. Several towns have risen up here, such as Los Barrios, Azofa and the island's capital, Valverde, home to a great number of people.

Santa María de Valverde, known by the indigenous people as Amoco, was declared the capital after the conquest and colonization by the Norman Jean de Bethencourt, at the beginning of the XV century, by the grace of the King of Castile, Henry III.

Its name (verde means green in Spanish) comes from the vegetation

◀ *Valverde. Church of the Conception.*

Panorama of Valverde.

63

Tower of the Church of the Conception, Valverde.

that covers the edges of the plateau on three sides. Much of this vegetation has now dissapeared or been substituted by other things, and brushwood and grazing land now predominate. Two important mountains situated close to the capital are Pedrera and Cuesta Cayetano.

When it became the capital, Valverde's inhabitants made their living from the grazing land. However, when the administrative, religous and military functions were organised, land used as pasture and agriculture were relegated to the rural areas. This transformation, or new way of life brought with it a

dominant social class and very soon commerce was established. When Valverde was declared the capital, its mayors took charge of civil and criminal jurisdiction. As a result, two social sectors were created, one situated in the city and the other in the rural area. The people in the city had strong economic power and established the powerful rule of the nobles, known as rabos blancos (white tails). The rest of the inhabitants of the island, the majority of which depended on them, were known as rabos negros (black tails).

Towards the middle of this century, the island contained a considerable number of inhabitants, but emigration cut away at the population, who headed towards the capitals of other islands of the archipelago or to other continents, especially America.

Valverde is surrounded by districts and hamlets. To the north they are spread out, and some of them, such as Las Montañetas, have very few inhabitants,

Valverde's Town Hall.

Panorama of San Andrés.

Parish Church of San Andrés.

Church of Mocanal. Detail.

Panorama of Mocanal.

◀ *Tamaduste.*

View of Tamaduste.

but they all live in moderate circumstances, always feeling the touch of the Trade Winds. Places such as Jarales, Guarazoca, Erese, Tesbado, Casas del Monte, Betenama and Mocanal-Tenecedra, that had a mayor's office that dealt with any small matter that might crop up, and Echedo. Their main activity or livelihood is based mainly on agriculture, with a variety of crops: potatoes, millet, grapes, etc.

The lower area of Los Barrios, from Salmor to Echedo, on the northern coast, is semi-arid, with various volcanic cones, where erosion has eaten away at the original features, making it almost unsuitable for cultivation. Due to negligence it is currently an area of brushwood and grazing land.

Las Calcosas Valley, with its saltpetrous ground. A flat area that hopes to be able to export its tropical products, constantly trying to adapt as irrigated lands, but with a lack of water for irrigation, for the water taken from the open well is never enough for the task

Around Tamaduste.

capital and airport; refuge of fishing vessels and a wonderful beach on which to laze the day away. Llano de los Cangrejos is situated in its southern region, and is where the airport is situated. Valverde and the area of Azofa in the far south, that occupy the western half of Nisdafe, up to the Azofa coast and its districts: Tiñor, San Andrés, Las Rosas, La Cuesta, Los Llanos, La Laja-La Torre, Tajace de Abajo, Isora. They are all located at an altitude that ranges from 800 m to 1 050 m.

The economic resourses of this area stem from the agrarian sector (potatoes, rye, fruit trees) and cattle rearing. The most remarkable ravines on the island, such as the one in Tiñor, are situated in the north of this area,

Punta Grande.

in hand. Echedo, the southern part of this valley. Echedo and its mountain, Tanganiscaba. Lands of rye and vineyards, that cover most of this area up to Tesoro mountain. Fig trees and mocanes, enveloped in everlasting loneliness. The dales of Los Barrios, speckled with millet and potatoes. Las Salinas mountain, whose slopes taper down to the sea, no longer home to the salting factories used to salt cheese. Pozo de Las Calcosas, with its outstanding traditional architecture, in harmony with the landscape of lava that decorates this part of the coast. Tamaduste cove, an important tourist centre because of its proximity to the

Loma del Toril.

Las Puntas.

from the south of Valverde to La Hondura. Various crops are grown on the fertile land in the little cauldron of Valverde. La Hondura Valley and Tiñor, with the Cumbrecita (Little Peak), and San Andrés which is protected by the mountains of Las Chamuscadas, Los Helechos and Entremontañas. Temirijaque Bay, on the southern coast of El Hierro, enveloped in everlasting silence. Houses scattered here and there, occasionally visited by wandering herds of goats. The sandy beaches of Azofa, sheltered by the sheer cliffs and tapering softly to the sea. The nostalgia of the constant move to new pastures along the narrow passes.

The Municipality of Valverde, with Los Lomos and Nisdafe. Nisdafe is situated to the northeast of the island, a plateau that stands between 900 and 1.100 m high, and thanks to the Trade Winds, is a wet area. In the XVII century, the mountanous area was ploughed and converted into communal pastures that existed until the XIX century. As the land is very fertile here, it has made a positive contribution to the economy. The edges of this plateau have permitted the creation of various centres of population. Nisdafe and Los Lomos, have always been closely linked and the land in both areas is dotted with holes made by volcanoes. Caldera de Ventaiga, in harmony with the Lomo (Ridge) de Ajonse and Ventejuí Peak. Lands of relics and legends. Areas that gave shelter to the revered Arbol Santo (Holy Tree). Jirdamas or tagastes (type of bush) cover the surface. The volcanos of Las Chamuscadas, Las Charquillas... Nisdafe, an area of pastures and agriculture, with its quiet hamlets: Hoya de la Vaca, La Albarda, El Corral Alto..

Valverde de El Hierro and its church, dedicated to Our Lady of the Conception. A three naved temple with buttresses outside and a two doored façade. The tower and temple date back to 1767. The interior is like a rich treasure, with its Barroque style, polychrome, high altarpiece, a polychrome statue of The Immaculate Conception, a polychrome Madonna by the Canarian school, an XVIII century Christ by the Genoese school, and a popular carving of el Señor de los Grillos. The silversmithing in the church is also worth mentioning, with an outstanding silver lamp and two silver chandeliers.

Valverde is a region of escarpments and hillocks, a coastal dreamland. Valverde with its lined streets and mixture of traditional and modern homes.

Valverde is Betenema, La Caleta, Casas del Monte, La Cuesta, Echedo, Erese, Guarazoca, Hoyo del Barrio, Isora and Jarales, Los Llanos, Mocanal, Las Montañetas, Puerto de la Estaca, Las Rosas, San Andrés, Tajace de Abajo, Tamaduste, Tesbabo, Tiñor and La Torre...

Frontera

From the capital of the island continue downwards, along the winding roads towards another municipality, passing through diverse landscapes, such as Tiñor or San Andrés, or the lands of Malpaso..., until you arrive at the municipality of Frontera.

Frontera has a surface area of 165,06 km^2 and a population of approximately 3 600, that occcupy the western half of the island, from El Pinar onwards. It has three separate regions: El Pinar and La Restinga, El Julán and La Dehesa and El Golfo. This municipality was formed after the political-administrative re-structuring of the island in 1911.

The hamlet of El Pinar is located on the island's southern most escarpment, from north to south from El Golfo, and to the west from Las Playas (The Beaches) to La Restinga. Its name (Frontera means border) originated from the predominant vegetation: pine trees, which form one of the most important areas of forrest in the Canary Islands. Pine trees are the dominant feature from the peak of Las Playas to El Julán. El Pinar's economic resources come from agriculture and cattle raising. The lower half is home to the largest of El Hierro's lava flows, and one of the most interesting in the whole archipelago: El Lajial. It is found between Naos by and Tecorón, and has been declared a Protected Area. As the land here is not suitable for agriculture and cattle rearing, it has an abundant vegetation, in close harmony with the rest of the landscape. An

Frontera. Panorama.

example of this is the Llano de Iramas. Some volcanic cones have been used as market gardens growing barley, rye, vines or dates. A clear example of this is the Hoya de Tecorón.

La Restinga is situated near the old port of Naos. Its inhabitants settled here round about the 1940's, and in subsequent decades it became very important as a result of the breakwater built as a shelter for the fishing boats and as a tourist centre.

The population of Taibique was the second largest on the island after Valverde. 1911 was a crucial year as regards the division of the island, for two municipalities were created. To the great disappointment of El Pinar, who had hoped to be named a municipal city, Frontera was chosen instead. El Pinar, Taibique and Las Casas were left out, for emigration was running rife in these towns.

Its economy is based on the rearing of sheep and goats, and transhumance is still practiced today. Subsistence

agriculture, based on cereals, potatoes and pod vegetables, with fruit trees dotted about here and there. Fig trees constitute the most important fruit, and are some of the best in the whole of El Hierro.

El Julán, situated in the lower half of the west of El Hierro, is not affected by the Trade Winds. Its climate is arid, and is therefore not cultivated, sheer escarpments constituting its most dominant feature. Large ravines criss-cross the whole area, which is engaged in a constant battle to keep the vegetation alive. It is a region lacking in human warmth and without cattle rearing or agricultural resources. To all

Another view of Frontera.

accounts, the most inhospitable and desolate area on the island. The coastal seaboard of El Julám, that streches from Tecorón to Punta Orchilla, is quite straight, and the ravines that taper out to the coast form small beaches. As they are sheltered by the notheast winds, the sea that laps at the shore is calm, and the coast here has therefore been called: Mar de las Calmas (Sea of Calms). In 1931 one of the most important lighthouses in the area of Orchilla was built. It was for a long time the point of reference of the Zero Meridian, until King Louis XIV started the custom of using the observatory of each country for this, which was how the one at Greenwich was selected. La Dehesa (meadow) gets its name from the communal land used as pasture, and is the most important grazing area in the whole archipelago. It is located in the extreme west of El Hierro, on a slope that descends softly to the west. Volcanic cones, with an almost total lack of vegetation due to the pasture land, pierce its surface, and the mountains of Tembárgena, and la

◀ *South Coast of El Hierro.*

Cape Orchilla.

View of Sabinosa.

Virgen, on whose side the hermitage of Los Reyes and Tenascas is situated, tower above the area.

Next to Letime, on el Verodal, to the northwest of La Dehesa, you will come accross the Sabinar, the distinguished remains of this type of vegetation. Constantly hit by the strong wind, the trunks grow in the direction it blows, many of which are so bent over that they touch the ground. The effect of the wind and cattle farming, have made parts of these lands totally barren.

In the peaks of La Dehesa, Sabinosa, the grazing land has been ploughed so that crops can be grown, such as potatoes, pod vegetables and various cereals. According to the chronicles, the governor, Lázaro Vizcaíno was killed in La Dehesa by Adamán, from El Hierro, who sought revenge for the crimes committed by this servant of Bethencourt.

This region is home to the hermitage dedicated to the Virgen de los Reyes (Virgen of the Kings), and dates back to 1576. The statue was abandoned on 6th January 1546, by the crew of a boat on its way to Cuba. It was taken by the villagers to Caracol cave, where they paid homage to it. The shepherds of this region declared her the Patron Saint and every year on the 25th of April celebrate her feast day. As a result of the miracles she works when there is a drought, the people from El Hierro pay homage to her, and every four years, she is brought down from the hermitage to Valverde. In September, La Dehesa celebrates the agricultural festivity, giving thanks for the abundant crops that have been harvested...

El Golfo is not only the most outstanding geographical accident of El Hierro, but also, the largest and best defined region. We can diferentiate between two zones: the eastern zone, which is the largest and most densely populated, and the western one, which is smaller and with fewer inhabitants. They are separated by the Tanganasoga mountain mass. In the

Hermitage of Virgen de los Reyes.

El Sabinar.

peaks, between Tanganasoga and Sabinosa, towards El Gretime, there is an important mass of monteverde. In El Tablado, thanks to the Trade Winds, there are fruit tree plantations: apple trees, fig trees, chestnuts, walnuts, osiers..., which grow close to other crops, such as maize, cereals and potatoes. To the west of the Riscos Bascos, you will come to the terraces of Arenas Blancas and El Verodal. This coastal region has prominant hills and rises in the land, La Puente being a good example of these.

Sabinosa, with a hamlet that has been well preserved, constituting an excellent example of traditional architecture, stands out in the region of El Golfo. It is 350 m high and its name originates from the numerous sabinas that grow here. It is an area of fig trees and vineyards, and has also suffered the effects of emigration.

The eastern part of El Golfo is flater, larger and very rich, shaped by el Valle (the Valley). It is an area of irrigation farming. Once over the 300 m mark, and at the foot of the largest depressions on the hill, lie the hamlets of

Llanillos, Merese, Las Toscas, Tigaday, Belgara Alta, Belgara Baja and Frontera, the municipal capital, situated on the sides of Guapira Mountain. It is also known as Las Lapas (limpets), due to an indigenous conchera found nearby. The best wines are produced in these lands. Other districts are los Mocanes, Guinea, Las Casillas and Las Puntas.

The Roques (hills) de Salmor are situated to the east of Las Puntas, and are inhabited by giant lizards that are more than 50 cm long. This spot has been declared a Protected Area.

Apart from the vineyards and fruit trees, El Golfo accepted the banana plantation as its own, which somewhat transformed the landscape here. It had its days of splendour, but the frequent storms decreased productivity and reduced the areas of cultivation. As a substitute tropical pineapple has been planted, with excellent results.

Frontera, municipal city, is situated on the hillside of Fuga de Gorreta; rising up on a large shelf beside various different plantations. The roads are straight and the buildings are almost piled up on top of each other. Frontera has a church dedicated to Nuestra Señora de la Candelaria (Our Lady of Candlemas), with a bell tower embedded into the top of a volcano and separated from the actual temple. It dates back to the year 1615. Inside there is a Madonna by the Canarian school, a carving of Saint John the Baptist, found in the bay of El Golfo in 1756 and a San Blas, by the popular school of art. Its silver work includes a Monstrance from America.

After observing the wonderful scenery, go back the way you came to Valverde. You will leave behind the hamlets, rocky areas, misterious mountains and pastures and a sea tinged with a thousand colours that has many a tale to tell. Tales of those who left never to return, or of those who went away but were brought back by the wonderful memories of their homeland.

BIBLIOGRAPHY

La Gomera paso a paso, Colectivo Raíz.

Atlas de Canarias,
Editorial Interinsular Canaria.

El Folclore musical en la isla de El Hierro,
Centro de la Cultura Popular Canaria.

Natura y cultura de las islas Canarias,
Editorial Interinsular Canaria.

Geografía de Canarias - Tomo 4,
Editorial Interinsular Canaria.

Los paisajes naturales de la isla de El Hierro, Centro de la Cultura Popular Canaria.

Etnografía y anales de la conquista de las islas Canarias, Ediciones Goya.

Historia de Canarias - Tomo I,
Editorial Planeta.

Historia del arte en Canarias,
Editorial Edirca.

Cocina de la isla de El Hierro (Alvarita Padrón), Centro de la Cultura Popular Canaria.

NEWSPAPER LIBRARY

Newspaper "Diario de Avisos", section "Paisajes y paisanajes canarios", Dr. Manuel Pérez Rodríguez.

We wish to express our warmest thanks to the Tourist Board off "Cabildo Insular" of El Hierro for all the information they supplied.

INDEX